ISBN: 97983751120768

Imprint: Independently published

Disclaimer: All answers are correct as of 31st May 2021.

Stenlake Publications presents:

Chelsea Crossword

Check out our other books:

Liverpool Crossword
Manchester United Crossword
Arsenal Crossword
Manchester City Crossword
Tottenham Hotspur Crossword
Leeds United Crossword
Newcastle United Crossword
Sunderland Crossword
Leicester City Crossword
Celtic Crossword
Rangers Crossword
England Crossword

"The club becomes you once you've played for it, you're always welcomed back for the rest of your life."

- Frank Lampard

"He's done it! The greatest night in the history of Chelsea Football Club! European Champions! They've beaten Bayern in their own backyard!"

- Martin Tyler

"You can take a player out of Chelsea, but you can never take Chelsea out of the player"

- Didier Drogba

Contents Page

Round 1 - Founding & History

Chelsea Football Club were founded in 1905 in Fulham. London and were named after the neighbouring borough as Fulham Football Club had already been founded 26 years earlier. This crossword covers the earliest decades of the club's history.

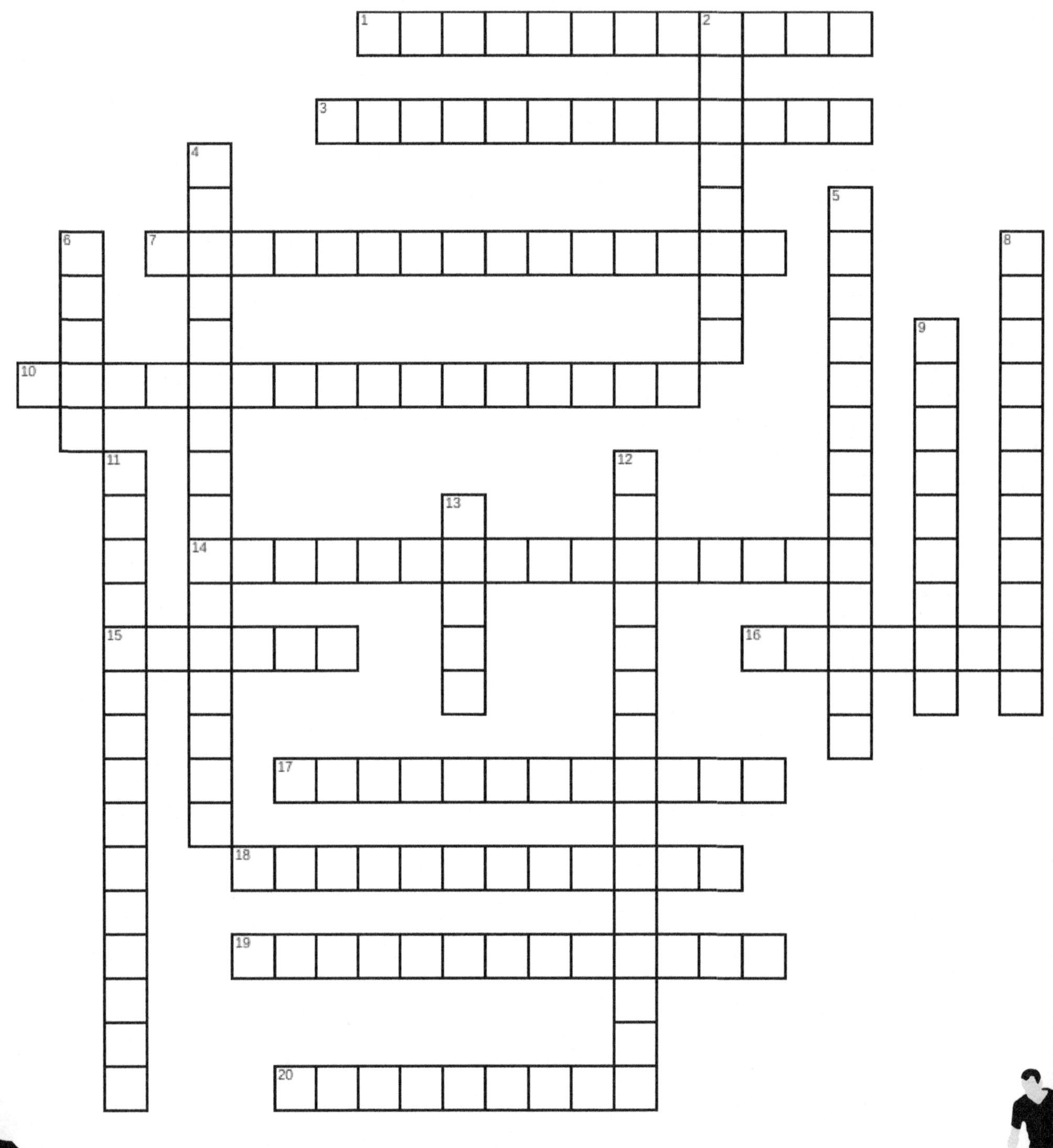

Across

1. Name of the pub (now known as The Butchers Hook) that the club was founded in. (3.6.3)

3. Nicknamed "Gatling Gun" and was the first player to score 100 goals for the club. (6.7)

7. Legendary manager at the helm from 1907-33. (5.10)

10. Prime minister who gave captain John Harris the Football League War Cup trophy. (7.9)

14. Fulham and this other London club rejected Chelsea's application to the Southern League. (9.7)

15. Club that the founder tried to persuade to move into Stamford Bridge but was unsuccessful over a rent dispute.

16. A club record and the second highest ever attendance at an English league match (82.905) came against this London side in 1935.

17. Manager from 1939-52 credited with developing the Chelsea youth and scouting system. (5.7)

18. Reigning champions of the Soviet Union who played Chelsea in a tour of the UK after WWII which drew in over 100.000 fans. (6.6)

19. 22 stone goalkeeper who was the club's first marquee signing. (7.6)

20. Legendary Manchester United manager . who made guest appearances for the club . during World War II. (4.5)

Down

2 Chelsea's founder. (3.5)

4. London club they made their Wembley debut against in the 1944 Football League War Cup Final. (8.8)

5. Scottish international player-manager who scored the club's first competitive goal. (4.9)

6. City that hosted the "Arts et Techniques dans la Vie moderne" in which Chelsea became the first English club ever to participate in an international tournament.

8. The first Chelsea player to score over 100 league goals and is the club's 8th highest goalscorer of all time. (6.5)

9. South American country Chelsea toured in 1929.

11. Their first FA Cup final. the so-called "Khaki" cup final at Old Trafford was against this opposition. (9.6)

12. Their first league game was a 1-0 loss against this Greater Manchester opposition. (9.6)

13. Original colour of the shorts.

Round 2 - 1950/60s

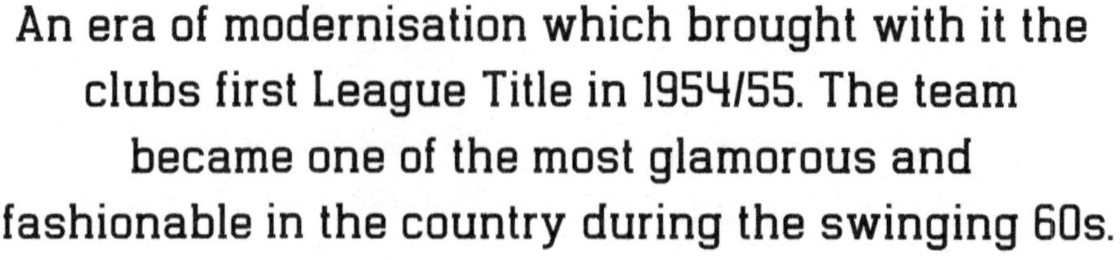

An era of modernisation which brought with it the clubs first League Title in 1954/55. The team became one of the most glamorous and fashionable in the country during the swinging 60s.

Across

2. Midfielder and future England manager who made 237 appearances for the club. (5.8)

4. Goalkeeper who made 729 appearances for the club over 19 seasons. (5.7)

6. Cheshire side, then of the fourth division, who knocked Chelsea out of the FA Cup in 1961. (5.9)

12. Midlands title rivals Chelsea dramatically done the double over in their title winning season including a 4-3 victory away having been 3-2 down going into stoppage time. (13.9)

14. Number of points secured in the 1954/55 title winning season - one of the lowest to have secured the English League title since the First World War. (5.3)

16. Manager Tommy Docherty had referred to his team as his "little ______" during a TV documentary and the name stuck.

17. Manager who replaced Tommy Docherty in 1967. (4.6)

18. North West club who Chelsea played in back-to-back FA Cup runs in 1965 and 1966.

19. England World Cup winner who scored 132 goals in 169 games before leaving for Milan. (5.7)

Down

1. One of the first "tracksuit managers" who used to shake each player by the hand and wish them "all the best" before each match. (3.5)

2. Team who defeated Chelsea in the first all-London FA Cup final, known as the Cockney Cup Final. (9.7)

3. Christian feast day that Chelsea beat Sheffield Wednesday on in 1955 to secure their first title. (2.7.3)

5. Tough defender nicknamed "chopper" who is Chelsea's all-time record appearance holder with 795. (3.6)

7. Full-back forced to retire at the age of 25 and later became manager in 1977. (3.8)

8. The club's old nickname before it was changed to "the blues" in the early 50s. (3.10)

9. Full back/Midfielder who holds the English record for most top flight appearances with 714 which included 436 with Chelsea. (4.7)

10. Italian side who Chelsea played in the Fairs Cup when their team bus was ambushed by opposition fans.

11. Second top goalscorer of all-time with 202 goals. (5.8)

13. Top goalscorer and captain who led Chelsea to the 1954/55 league title. (3.7)

15. Animal introduced as the new crest.

Round 3 - 1970/80s

The majority of this period was one of decline. An ambitious redevelopment of Stamford Bridge threatened the financial stability of the club, star players were sold and the team were relegated three times.

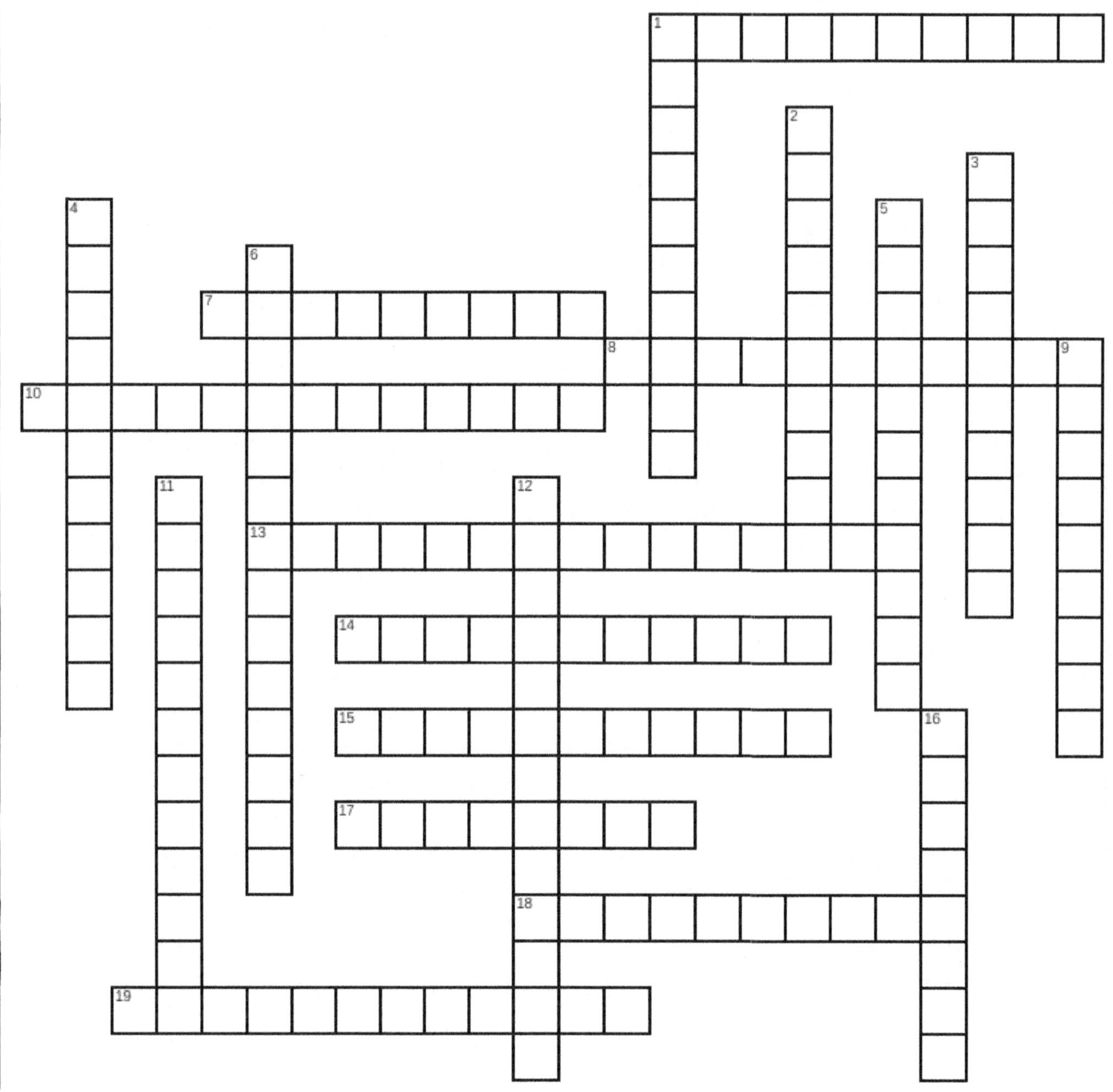

Across

1. Chelsea beat Jeunesse Hautcharage from this nation, 21-0 on aggregate in a Cup Winners' Cup Final tie, a record score line in European competition.

7. Development of this stand was one of the main causes of Chelsea's financial problems in the 1970s and 1980s. (4,5)

8. Legendary player appointed manager in 1985. (4,7)

10. Manager appointed in 1988. (5,8)

13. Scored 24 goals in the 1976/77 season. (5,10)

14. Scored a crucial last-minute winner in the penultimate game of the 1982/83 season to save the club from relegation to the third tier. (5,6)

15. Lincolnshire side that Chelsea took 10,000 fans on the final day of the 1983/84 season. (7,4)

17. Businessman who bought the club for £1 in 1981. (3,5)

18. Striker signed from Reading who scored 36 goals in the 1983/84 season. (5,5)

19. Stadium that Chelsea nearly ground shared at after a club dispute over Stamford Bridge. (8,4)

Down

1. A merger was proposed between Fulham and Queens Park Rangers so that Chelsea could relocate to this stadium in the 80s. (6,4)

2. 1966 World Cup final hero who became manager in September 1979. (5,5)

3. Midfielder appointed captain at 18 and would later become assistant manager in two separate spells. (3,7)

4. Scot signed from Hibernian for £300,000 in 1986 who went onto to score 63 goals in 179 appearances. (6,5)

5. Disruptive or unlawful behaviour such as rioting, bullying and vandalism, usually in connection with crowds at sporting events.

6. Team defeated in the inaugural Full Members Cup Final. (10,4)

9. Staffordshire side who defeated Chelsea against the odds in the 1972 League Cup Final. (5,4)

11. Scottish international forward who scored 64 goals in 205 games for Chelsea in the 80s. (5,7)

12. Midfielder signed from Bournemouth for £35,000 and eventually sold to Liverpool 4 years later after 141 league appearances. (5,8)

16. Manager appointed in 1983 which marked a turn in fortunes for the club. (4,4)

Round 4 - 1990s

A period which began with a return to the top flight and finished with a FA Cup, League Cup, Cup Winners' Cup and Super Cup. An Italian renaissance began in the late 90s and they were joined by other international players from the continent to give the side a new image.

Across

2. Talented Romanian full-back signed for £2.3 million. (3.8)

3. 1970 FA Cup winner who took over as caretaker manager in 1993. (5.4)

6. Club that Gianfranco Zola scored a back-heel goal against in 2002. (7.4)

7. The only player in European footballing history to have both winners and runners up medals in all three main European club competitions. (8.6)

8. Spanish side defeated in the 1998 UEFA Super Cup. (4.6)

10. Scored in the first minute of the 1997 FA Cup Final. (7.2.6)

12. Republic of Ireland midfielder and former ITV co-commentator who made 138 appearances for the club. (4.8)

13. Cultured French World Cup winning defender. (5.7)

14. North east club defeated in their second Full Members Cup Final.

16. Dutch legend signed on a free transfer from Sampdoria and was player manager from 1996-98. (4.6)

17. South African-born striker. nicknamed "The Golden One". (4.5)

18. German side defeated in the 1998 Cup . Winners' Cup Final.

Down

1. Dutch goalkeeper who set the record for most clean sheets in a season (27) until it was broken by Petr Cech. (2.2.3)

2. 5ft 6in midfielder signed from the crazy gang for a club record £1.6 million. (6.4)

4. Manager from 1991-93. (3.11)

5. Spanish side and eventual winners of the 1993/94 Cup Winners' Cup who knocked Chelsea out in the semi-finals. (4.8)

9. Popular director and financial benefactor who died in a helicopter crash following a League Cup match against Bolton Wanderers. (7.7)

11. Player/manager from 1993-96 who left to become England manager. (5.6)

14. Welshman signed for £1.5 million in 1995. (4.6)

15. First Uruguayan to play for Chelsea. (3.5)

Round 5 - 2000s

It was after the arrival of a billionaire owner that Chelsea became a powerhouse in England and in Europe. A flurry of big money signings and the arrival of Jose Mourinho brought back-to-back Premier League titles. Three FA Cups and two League Cups were also won in the 2000s.

Across

3. Club that William Gallas was signed from.

4. English team that Chelsea faced 10 times in the Champions League this decade including three semi-final ties in four years.

5. Scored a hat-trick in a 5-0 win over Sunderland in 2009. (7.6)

8. Irish winger signed from Blackburn Rovers in 2003. (6.4)

10. Scored first ever FA Cup Final winner at the new Wembley. (6.6)

12. Russian-Israeli billionaire businessman and politician who bought the club from Ken Bates in 2003. (5.10)

14. Club that Chelsea secured the 2004/05 title at. (6.9)

18. Team defeated in the 2000 FA Cup Final. (5.5)

19. Argentine loaned to Inter and AC Milan during his time at Chelsea and scored a Champions League Final brace. (6.6)

20. Chelsea were temporarily banned from signing players for two years after a contract breach to sign this young Frenchman. The decision was later overturned. (4.6)

Down

1. Only Cameroonian to make 100+ appearances for Chelsea.

2. They won the League Cup by beating this team in the last ever English cup final at the Millennium Stadium.

6. Midfielder so good, he has a position named after him. (6.8)

7. Legendary Dutch scout responsible for bringing Ronaldo and Romario to PSV that was brought in, considered one of the greatest ever. (4.2.6)

9. Portuguese centre-back who made 210 appearances for the club. (7.8)

11. Scored Chelsea's goal in the 2008 Champions League Final. (5.7)

13. Manager appointed in 2004. (4.8)

15. Club that Frank Lampard and Joe Cole were signed from. (4.3.6)

16. Israeli appointed manager in 2007. (5.5)

17. Team memorably beaten 6-4 on aggregate in a 2005 Champions League last-16 tie.

Round 6 – 2010s

The most successful decade in the club's history as two more Premier League titles, three FA Cups, a League Cup were won domestically. The club's greatest night came in 2012 as they won the elusive Champions League trophy and followed that up with a Europa League victory in 2013.

Across

4. Scored a brace at Southampton to complete a comeback from 2-0 down in 2018. (7.6)

10. Zaire-born Portuguese international right-back who also played for QPR. (4.8)

11. Manager appointed in June 2011. (5.6.4)

12. Won back-to-back player of the year awards in 2012 and 2013. (4.4)

13. Scored an injury time winner in the 2013 Europa League Final. (9.8)

14. Chelsea's top goalscorer in the 2010/11 Premier League season. (7.7)

15. Colombian striker signed on loan from Monaco. (7.6)

18. Top goalscorer in three consecutive seasons from 2014-2017. (5.5)

19. Player who has won La Liga. Copa del Rey. Champions League. Super Cup. Club World Cup. Premier League. FA Cup. Europa League. the Euros and World Cup.

20. Brazilian signed despite him completing a medical at Spurs.

Down

1. Club who defeated Chelsea in the 2012 Club World Cup Final.

2. The 2017/18 season saw Chelsea sign their most lucrative commercial deal in their history by signing with this kit manufacturer.

3. Won a club record four player of the year awards. (4.6)

5. Goalkeeper signed for a world record fee in 2018. (4.12)

6. Top goalscorer in all competitions in the 2012/13 season. (8.6)

7. Eden Hazard score the Premier League's April 2019 goal of the month with a solo effort against this team. (4.3.6)

8. Team defeated 8-0 on the final day of the 2009/10 season. (5.8)

9. Club Chelsea secured the 2015/16 title with Hazard scoring the winner in a 1-0 win. (7.6)

16. Side defeated in the 2012 Club World Cup semi-final.

17. Goalkeeper who made 20 Premier League appearances between 2006-2014.

Round 7 - Champions League 2012 & 2021

Chelsea's two greatest nights in their history came in 2012 and 2021 as they were crowned Champions of Europe. How much can you remember about these two unforgettable Champions League campaigns?

Across

2. Host stadium of the 2012 Final. (7.5)

3. Original host city of the 2021 Final.

4. Man of the match in the 2021 Final. (5.5)

6. Spaniard who came on as a sub against Bayern. (8.6)

9. Scored the winner at the Estádio da Luz in the 2012 Quarter-final first leg. (7.5)

11. Host stadium of the 2021 Final. (7.2.6)

13. Team that Chelsea beat in the round of 16 in 2021. (8.6)

15. Assisted the 2021 Final winning goal. (5.5)

16. German side in Chelsea's 2011/12 group. (5.10)

17. Nationality of the officiating team for the 2021 Final.

18. Took and scored Bayern's third penalty in the shoot-out. (6.5)

19. English stadium that offered to step in and host the 2021 Final after Covid-19 travel restrictions were enforced. (5.4)

20. Man of the match in the 2012 Final (6.6)

Down

1. Scored the winning goal in the 2021 Final. (3.7)

5. Player who clashed with Kevin de Bruyne which forced him off injured. (7.7)

7. Player who had a penalty saved by Petr Čech in extra time. (5.6)

8. Team in Bayern's group which Chelsea beat in the round of 16 in 2012.

10. First player to score a penalty for Chelsea in the shoot-out. (5.4)

12. Defender injured in the 39th minute of the 2021 Final. (6.5)

14. Club who both Chelsea's Final opponents played on their route to the Final.

Round 8 - José Mourinho

Arguably the clubs greatest ever manager. José won three Premier League's, three League Cups and a FA Cup over his two spells at the club. He is considered a club legend and one of the greatest managers of all time.

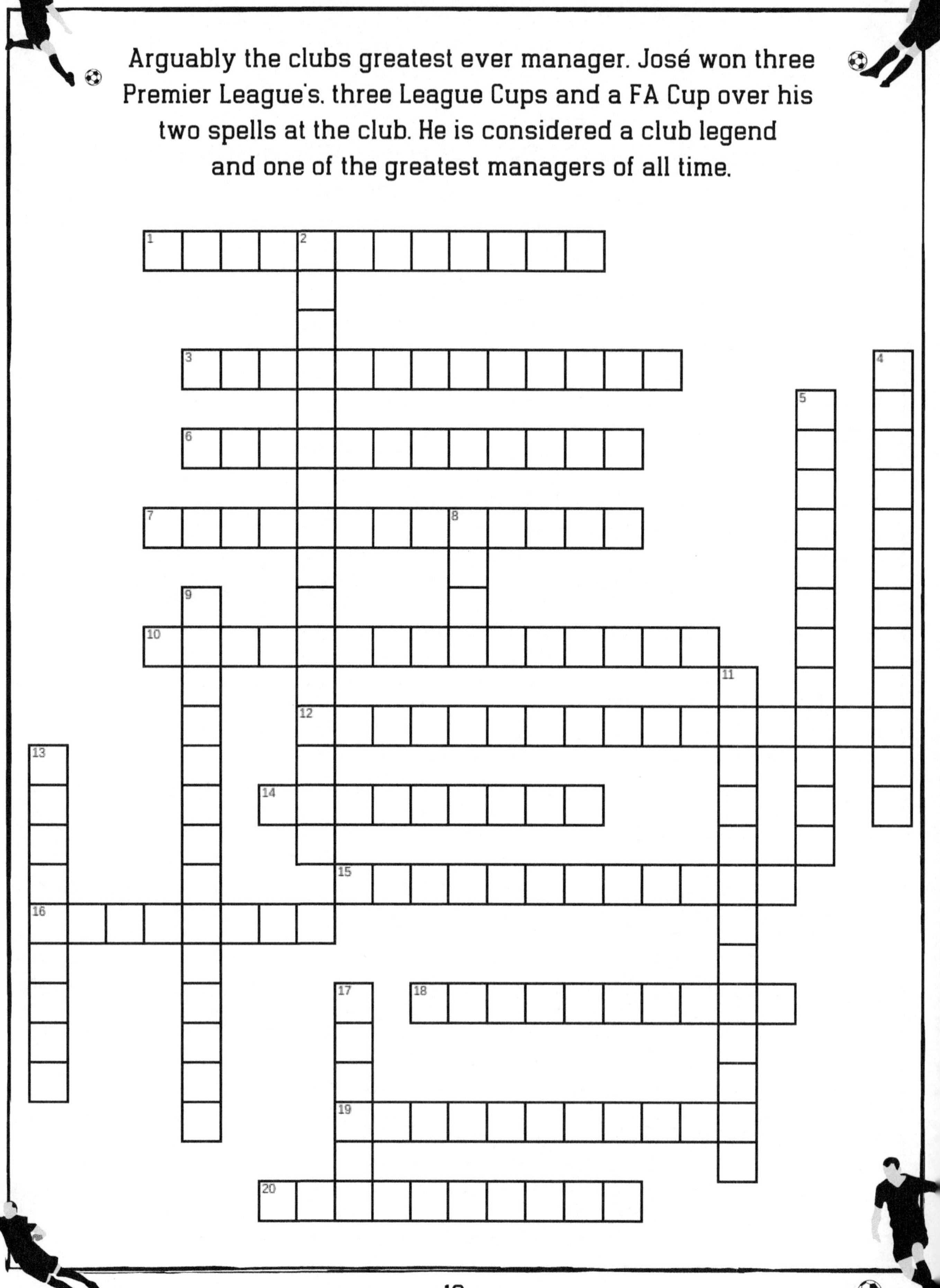

Across

1. Dutch coach he worked with at Barcelona. (5.3.4)

3. In 2014. he described this team as playing "19th century football". (4.3.6)

6. Chelsea player Mourinho signed for Manchester United in 2017. (7.5)

7. Right-back he bought with him from Porto. (5.8)

10. Centre-back he bought with him from Porto. (7.8)

12. Striker signed in 2006 that proved to be a point of contention between Jose and Abramovich. (6.10)

14. Premier League club he was offered the position of assistant manager in 2000.

15. Two-time Champions League winning manager he replaced at Benfica in his first manager role. (4.8)

16. Coach who has worked with Mourinho for 17 years. (3.5)

18. Club he won the treble with in 2009/10. (5.5)

19. Manager that Mourinho was interpreter for at Sporting Lisbon and Porto and assistant manager at Barcelona. (5.6)

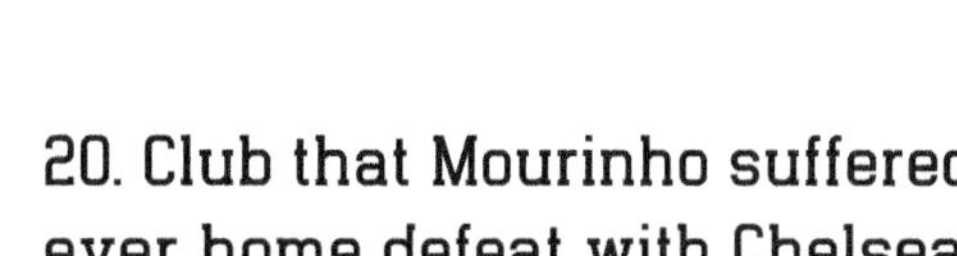

20. Club that Mourinho suffered his first . ever home defeat with Chelsea against.

Down

2. Stadium that Mourinho won his second Champions League at and would later become his home stadium. (8.8)

4. In the final of the 2011 Supercopa de España. Mourinho was seen gouging the eye of this Barcelona's assistant coach ______ during a brawl at the end of the game. (4.8)

5. Manager he described as "a voyeur". (6.6)

8. Club he took over in 2021.

9. National team captain he signed on a free from Bayern Munich in 2006. (7.7)

11. Nickname the media gave Mourinho following his first press conference as Chelsea's manager. (3.7.3)

13. He secured his first trophy at Chelsea by winning the League Cup against this team 3-2 (AET) in Cardiff.

17. He was born in a suburb of this city.

Round 9 - Italian Managers

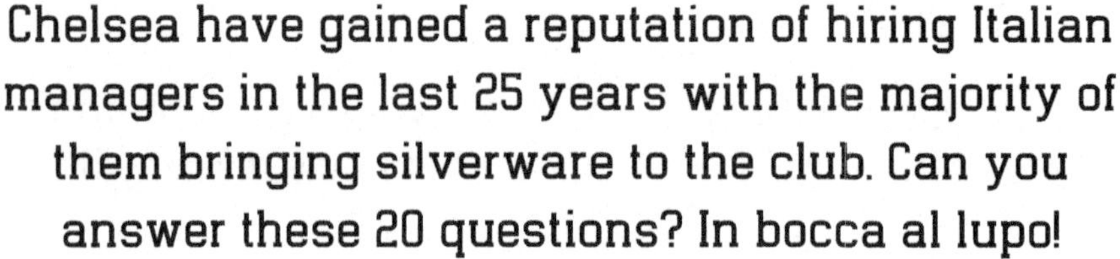

Chelsea have gained a reputation of hiring Italian managers in the last 25 years with the majority of them bringing silverware to the club. Can you answer these 20 questions? In bocca al lupo!

Across

1. Gianluca Vialli became the youngest ever manager to win a UEFA competition by winning this trophy. (3.7.3)

4. Manager often seen chewing on cigarette butts while on the touchline. (8.5)

6. Credited with bringing back and popularizing the 3-5-2 formation after it had seen very limited use since its heyday at the 1990 World Cup. (7.5)

7. Manager in between Ancelotti and Di Matteo. (5.6.4)

9. Club that Roberto Di Matteo was manager of before joining Chelsea as assistant manager. (4.8.6)

10. Antonio Conte's first major signing with Chelsea. (5.9)

12. Chelsea's first Italian (and second ever foreign) manager. (8.6)

13. Manager who made the most appearances as a player for the club. (7.2.6)

15. Club that Ancelotti. Conte and Sarri have all managed other than Chelsea.

16. Maurizio Sarri's profession whilst an amateur player in his youth.

17. Ranieri's most expensive signing as Chelsea's manager. (6.4)

18. Ancelotti led Chelsea to its first ever domestic double by defeating this team in the FA Cup final.

19. Team that Sarri beat in the Europa League Final to win his only trophy at Chelsea.

Down

1. Manager who picked up the nickname "The Tinkerman" after being accused of over rotating his squad. (7.8)

2. Manager who had the third highest win percentage in Premier League history at the time he left. (5.9)

3. Club that Conte beat in the 2018 FA Cup Final. (10.6)

5. The only non-Italian manager (other than José) to win a trophy between 2009-2019. (6.7)

8. Carlo Ancelotti's most expensive signing in his first transfer window as Chelsea's. . manager. (4.7)

11. Midfielder Maurizio Sarri brought with him from Napoli.

14. Club that Ranieri won the Premier League with.

Round 10 - Frank Lampard

The club's all-time leading goalscorer and one of the club's greatest players. Frank Lampard won three Premier League titles, four FA Cups, two League Cups, a Champions League and Europa League in his 13 seasons at the club.

Across

2. Player he overtook to become Chelsea's all-time leading goalscorer (5.8)

5. Prestigious secondary school he attended.

6. Name of his autobiography published in 2006. (7.5)

9. Club he began his career at. (4.3.6)

11. MLS club he played for. (3.4.4)

13. Name of his second wife. (9.8)

16. His first signing as Chelsea's manager. (5.6)

19. Name of his father.

20. Nation he made his England debut against.

Down

1. First managerial job. (5.6)

3. His one away Premier League hat-trick came against this North West club. (6.9)

4. Manager who gave him his professional debut. (5.8)

7. Club he scored a brace against to equal and beat the all-time club scoring record. (5.5)

8. His cousin who is a former England international and played for Liverpool and Spurs. (5.8)

10. Player whose deflected shot rebounded to Lampard to finish in the 2008 Champions League Final. (7.6)

12. He scored his first Premier League hat-trick against this Midlands club in 2008. (5.6)

14. Club he was loaned to in 1995. (7.4)

15. Large Essex (now East London) town he was born in.

17. Club he scored a 20-yard chip against in 2008 which Luiz Felipe Scolari described as he "best goal I have seen". (4.4)

18. Club he beat in the Championship play-off semi-finals as manager.

Round 12 - Stamford Bridge

Chelsea's home for their entire history. Stamford Bridge has seen many great moments through the years despite an expansion nearly bankrupting the club in the 1970s. The club have plans to expand capacity to 60,000 by the 2023-24 season.

Across

2. Stamford Bridge was designed by this famous football architect who developed many of the great UK stadiums during the 20th century. (9.6)

4. Street that Stamford Bridge is located on. (6.4)

5. Former American football team who called Stamford Bridge home in 1997. (6.8)

6. Closest other professional football stadium to Stamford Bridge. (6.7)

10. The oldest independent track and field club in the world who were Stamford Bridge's first tenants from 1877-1904. (6.8.4)

15. Closest London Underground station on the Piccadilly Line. (5.5)

16. Opponents in the last England international at Stamford Bridge in 1946.

17. Named of the south stand. (4.3)

18. South American side who played Russia in the last international held at Stamford Bridge in 2013.

Down

1. Former director that the North Stand is named after. (7.7)

3. Yorkshire side who played in two of the three FA Cup Finals held at Stamford Bridge. (12.4)

4. Nearest tube station to Stamford Bridge. (6.8)

7. The ashes of this legendary striker are under a penalty spot. (5.6)

8. Closest bus stop. (6.5)

9. Scotsman who has an executive box named after him. (5.6)

11. 5ft 5 in midfielder who was the last player to score at Stamford Bridge in the 20th century. (4.6)

12. Name of the report which recommended that football stadiums become all-seaters.

13. AC Milan loanee who scored the first Chelsea goal at Stamford Bridge in the 21st century. (6.4)

14. The record attendance of 82.905 came against this side in 1935.

17. Postcode.

Round 11 - John Terry

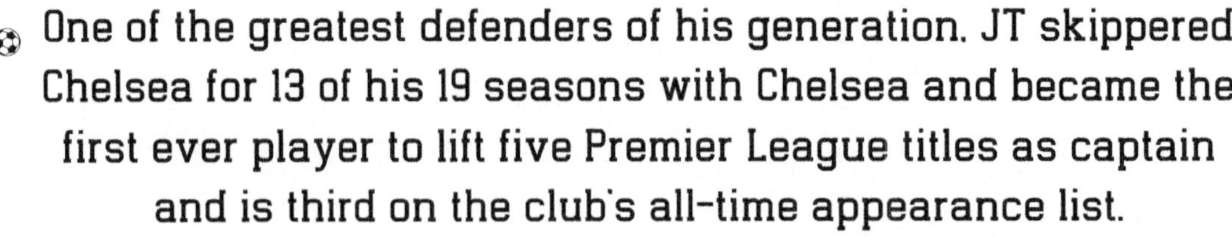

One of the greatest defenders of his generation. JT skippered Chelsea for 13 of his 19 seasons with Chelsea and became the first ever player to lift five Premier League titles as captain and is third on the club's all-time appearance list.

Across

2. Russian club he had a medical with in 2018 but ultimately turned down for family reasons. (7.6)

3. He scored Chelsea's fastest-ever goal in the Champions League by heading in a goal after 90 seconds against this German side.

5. French international. he partnered at centre-back in his early years in the Chelsea first team. (6.8)

9. Club he finished his career at and became assistant manager of in 2018. (5.5)

12. Club he was loaned to in 2000. (10.6)

13. Club he played in goal against in 2006.

14. Terry scored a FA Cup semi-final winner in 2002 against this London club.

18. Arsenal player who accidentally kicked Terry in the face in the 2007 League Cup Final leaving him unconscious for several minutes. (4.5)

19. Brazilian layer he appeared on the Pro Evolution Soccer 6 front cover with.

20. Manager who gave Terry the captaincy. (4.8)

Down

1. Club he supported as a boy. (10.6)

4. He scored England's first ever goal at the new Wembley against this nation.

6. Barcelona player he kneed and received a red card for violent conduct in the 2012 Champions League semi-final 2nd leg. (6.7)

7. Famous Sunday league side he played for in his youth.

8. His main centre-back partner during his England career. (3.9)

10. He made his last Chelsea appearance against this club and received a guard of honour when he was subbed in the 26th minute.

11. England manager that named him captain. (5.8)

15. Eastern European Nation he scored his only competitive England goal against.

16. District of East London he was born in.

17. Terry was the third best passer in world football in 2011 behind Swansea's Leon Brittan and this player.

Round 13 - Academy Graduates

The Chelsea academy is renowned around the world for producing great talents. Can you name this select group of 20 players?

Across

2. Defender who won the Premier League with Blackburn and went on to play for West Ham and Fulham. (3.6)

4. The club's most successful captain. leading them to five Premier League titles. four FA Cups. three League Cups. one Europa League and a Champions League title. (4.5)

5. Scotsman who made 113 league appearances for the club between 1989 and 1997. (5.6)

8. Became the youngest Chelsea player to score in the Champions League knockout stage by scoring against Porto in 2021. (5.5)

10. Scored 15 Premier League goals in 34 appearances for Chelsea in the 2019/20 season. (5.7)

12. Centre-back who spent five seasons out on loan to QPR and Wolves before joining Hamburg. (7.9)

14. Jamaican international defender who made 218 appearances between 1990-1998. (5.8)

16. Jersey-born left-back who made 312 appearances for the club over two spells. (6.2.4)

17. London-born Turkish international who played for Leicester and Birmingham. (5.5)

18. Dutch international who has commanded over £60 million in transfer fees through his career so far. (6.3)

19. Striker best known for his time at West Ham after making his Chelsea debut in 2002. (7.4)

20. Canadian-born England international loaned to AC Milan in 2021. (6.6)

Down

1. German centre-back who won three Premier League titles with two different clubs. (6.4)

3. Defender who made over 300 appearances for West Brom between 2000 and 2010. (4.7)

6. Brazilian who was the only academy graduate given a debut by Di Matteo. (5.6)

7. Midfielder best known for his time at Everton and Charlton Athletic. (6.7)

9. Started left wing in the 2012 Champions League Final. (4.8)

11. Centre-back who played Premier League appearances for Chelsea. Leeds and Reading. (7.7)

13. Midfielder who has made 80+ Premier League appearances for Burnley. Swansea and Southampton. (4.5)

15. Right-back who scored his first Premier League goal. in a 3-1 win for Chelsea against Brighton & Hove Albion in September 2020. (5.5)

Round 14 - Club Captains

The club have had many legendary captains in their history. Can you name the last 20 based on their years as captain as well as the number of appearances and goals for the club?

1 2 3 4 5 6 7 8 9 10 11 12 13 14 15 16 17 18 19 20

Across

4. 1964-66 - 237 apps. 31. (5.8)

6. 1990-91 - 93 apps. 2 goals. (5.8)

7. (4VC) 2020- 216 apps. 11 goals and counting. (5.5)

8. 2001-04. 222 apps. 7 goals. (6.8)

11. 2019-. 425 apps. 14 goals. (5.11)

14. 1966-80 - 795 apps. 14 goals. (3.6)

17. (3VC) 2020- 30 apps. 2 goals and counting. (6.5)

18. 1953-56 - 367 apps. 152 goals. (3.7)

19. 1991-93. 138 apps. 12 goals. (4.8)

20. 1980-84 - 313 apps. 19 goals. (5.4)

Down

1. 1957-59 - 223 apps. 9 goals. (5.8)

2. 1959-64 - 347 apps. 54 goals. (5.9)

3. (VC) 2006-14. 648 apps. 211 goals. (5.7)

5. 1993-2001. 445 apps. 76 goals. (6.4)

9. 1988-90 - 83 apps. 22 goals. (6.7)

10. 1956-57 - 402 apps. 30 goals. (3.9)

12. 1984-88 - 346 apps. 10 goals. (5.5)

13. 2004-17. 717 apps. 67 goals. (4.5)

15. 2017-19. 290 apps. 25 goals. (4.6)

16. (VC) 2019-. 137 apps. 16 goals and counting.

Round 15 - Didier Drogba

Club legend Didier Drogba is the club's highest scoring foreign player and fourth top goalscorer of all-time. He won two Premier League golden boots and is the only player to score in four FA Cup Finals. His most iconic moment was the winning penalty in the 2012 Champions League Final.

Across

4. Drogba became the first African player to score 100 Premier League goals by netting against this side. (5.4)

10. Club Chelsea signed him from for £24 million in 2004.

14. Chinese side he played for. (8.7)

15. National team he scored 65 goals in 105 caps for. (5.5)

16. MLS team he played for. (8.6)

18. Assisted his equaliser in the 2012 Champions League Final from a corner. (4.4)

19. Club he won a European League title with (other than Chelsea).

20. Drogba became the first player to score in four different FA Cup Finals, as he netted the winner in Chelsea's 2-1 triumph over this side. (5.4)

Down

1. His first Premier League hat-trick came against this club in 2006.

2. Goalkeeper he left standing after a chest, turn and thunderous volley from the edge of the box in September 2006. (4.5)

3. His final appearance for Chelsea came against this club, where he was captain and was carried off by his teammates when substituted.

5. He scored his first Chelsea goal against this club. (8.6)

6. Club he scored a hat-trick against in an 8-0 win in May 2010. (5.8)

7. He played with this player at Guingamp and Chelsea. (7.7)

8. Goalkeeper he scored the Champions League winning penalty against. (6.5)

9. Legend he overtook to become number 14 on Chelsea's all-time record appearance holder. (5.6)

11. Club he turned professional at as a 21-year-old. (2.4)

12. Drogba scored his country's first ever World Cup goal against this South American nation.

13. Stadium he scored a stunning 35-yarder in the 87th minute on the 18th of December 2006. (8.4)

17. Disease that kept him out for a month in late 2010.

Round 16 - Gianfranco Zola

Gianfranco Zola, voted Chelsea's greatest ever player in a 2003 fan poll was one of the first great foreign players to represent the club. He won a Cup Winners' Cup, Super Cup, two FA Cups and a League Cup in seven seasons.

Across

2. Former Chelsea manager he played under at Parma. (5.9)

3. Manager who signed him for Chelsea. (4.6)

5. Chelsea manager he was assistant under. (8.5)

6. Icelandic player whose presence limited Zola's first team appearances in his later years at Chelsea. (5.10)

8. His shirt number at Chelsea that hasn't been worn since. (6.4)

10. Argentine he was understudy to at Napoli. (5.8)

12. Legendary Italian manager who gave him his national team debut. (6.6)

13. English club he managed from 2012-13.

15. Club Chelsea beat in the 1997 FA Cup Final to secure his first trophy with the club.

18. First managerial job. (4.3.6)

19. Club he scored a curling free kick against in the 1999/00 Champions League quarter-final.

20. Club he scored the winning goal against in the 1998 Cup Winners' Cup Final.

Down

1. Manager he played under at Napoli and Chelsea. (7.8)

4. Opposition manager who called him a "clever little so-and-so." (4.8)

7. Club he finished his career at and won promotion to Serie A with.

9. Club Chelsea signed him from.

11. Mediterranean island he was born on.

14. He scored his one Chelsea hat-trick against this club in 1997. (5.6)

16. His final competitive appearance for the club came against this club.

17. Zola scored his final goal for Chelsea, a lob from outside the penalty area against this club.

Round 17 - Eden Hazard

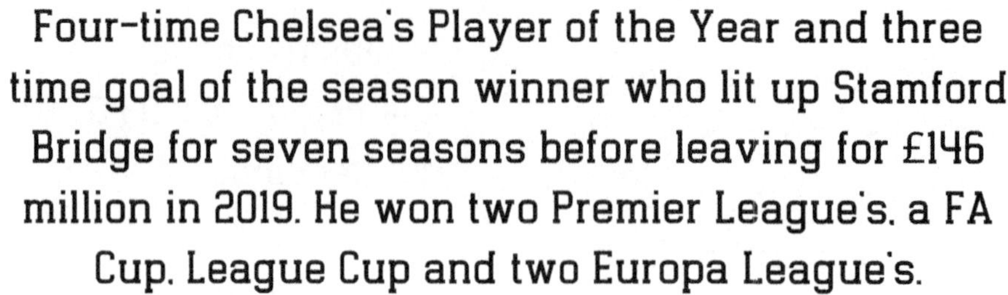

Four-time Chelsea's Player of the Year and three time goal of the season winner who lit up Stamford Bridge for seven seasons before leaving for £146 million in 2019. He won two Premier League's, a FA Cup, League Cup and two Europa League's.

Across

2. Player who he assisted in scoring his 200th Chelsea goal. (5.7)

7. Hazard was given the number 17 shirt previously worn by this player. (4.8)

8. Club where a kicked a ball boy in a League Cup semi-final tie. (7.4)

9. His last game for Chelsea was against this club.

10. Hazard won his first FA Cup in 2018 after scoring the winner against this side. (10.6)

11. He scored the decisive penalty against this side to send Chelsea into the 2019 Europa League Final. (9.9)

14. Hazard was instrumental as Belgium became the first team in 52 years to come back from 0-2 down to win a World Cup knockout match which came against this side.

16. His idol growing up was "watching him on television and online for hours." (8.6)

18. Club he scored his first Premier League hat-trick against in March 2014.

19. Nation he scored against in the 3rd place game at the 2018 World Cup.

20. Name of his brother who is a fellow Belgium international.

Down

1. In February. Hazard was scrutinised when he said it would "be difficult to say no" to a move to this side. (5.5.7)

3. Club he scored his 100th Chelsea and 150th career goal against.

4. Goalkeeper who was Hazard's teammate at Chelsea. Real Madrid and the national team. (7.8)

5. He scored a memorable solo winner in the third round of the EFL Cup at this stadium on 26 September 2018.

6. He was the first player to win back-to-back Ligue 1 player of the year awards since this former PSG and Portugal striker.

12. He became the first player since this Frenchman to record at least 15 goals and 15 assists in a Premier League season. (7.5)

13. Club he scored his last Premier League hat-trick against in September 2018. (7.4)

15. He was the first player to win back-to-back Chelsea player of the season awards since this player. (4.4)

17. Club he won a Ligue 1 title with before joining Chelsea.

Round 18 - General I

You've done well to reach this point: I hope you have learn't lots of cool facts about the blues. Here are three rounds of general questions from a range of categories to finish off. Good luck!

Across

4. Australian-born England international defender who played for Chelsea between 1987-91. (4.6)

5. Only player to win the CONCACAF Gold Cup whilst a Chelsea player. (4.6)

6. Second highest appearing African for the club. (4.3.5)

8. First player to win the Copa América as a Chelsea player.

9. Club that Ramires was sold to. (7.6)

10. Former Liverpool. Spurs and England striker who was forced to watch Chelsea as a youngster despite being a QPR fan. (5.6)

11. German side in Chelsea's Champions League group in 2011/12. (5.10)

13. Former Soccer AM presenter who is a lifelong Chelsea fan. (3.7)

16. Chairman since 2003. (5.4)

18. Two-time assistant manager who played for the club between 1990 and 1999. (5.6)

19. Chelsea's first ever European match was against BK Frem who are from this country.

Down

1. Side that Chelsea lost to in the 2003/04 Champions League semi-final.

2. Player who has scored the most penalties for the club. (5.7)

3. Foreign player who has made the most appearances for Chelsea. (4.4)

7. British side Chelsea beat in the 1970/71 Cup Winners' Cup semi-final. (10.4)

11. Highest ever fee paid for an Englishman. (3.8)

12. Name of the club's team doctor from 2009-15. (3.8)

14. Third top goalscorer of all-time. (5.5)

15. Wimbledon legend who kept net for Chelsea between 1989 and 1993. (4.7)

17. Host city of the 2021 Champions League Final.

Round 19 - General II

Across

3. In the mid-1970s, the away strip was a red, white and green kit inspired by this great national side of the 1950s.

4. Top goalscorer in the 1999-00 season. (4,5,3)

7. First player to score a Premier League hat-trick for Chelsea. (5,7)

9. Only Chelsea member of the England 1966 World Cup Winning Squad. (5,7)

10. A 2004 survey by Planetfootball.com found that Chelsea fans consider their main rivals to be this side.

11. Highest goal scoring European (ex England) in the club's history. (4,6)

12. Two-time winner of the Confederations Cup whilst at Chelsea. (6,8)

14. Chelsea player who was part of the 2014 World Cup winning squad. (5,8)

16. Side beaten in the 2012/13 Europa League semi-final.

17. Scored the most international goals whilst being a Chelsea player. (6,6)

18. Host stadium of the 1970 FA Cup Final replay. (3,8)

19. Player who has been out on six loan spells since signing from Wigan Athletic in 2012. (6,5)

Down

1. At Tommy Docherty's behest, in the 1966 FA Cup semi-final they wore blue and black stripes, based on this side's kit. (5,5)

2. Former US President who used to visit Stamford Bridge frequently whilst studying at Oxford University. (4,7)

5. Club that defeated the women's side in the 2020/21 Champions League Final.

6. Scored Chelsea's first away hat-trick in a 6-0 win at Barnsley in 1997. (8,6)

7. Host country of the 1971 Cup Winners' Cup Final.

8. Five-time Olympic Gold Medallist in rowing who is a lifelong supporter. (5,8)

13. Most appearances in UEFA competitions. (4,5)

15. Player who has been top goalscorer most times for Chelsea with 8. (3,7)

Round 20 - General III

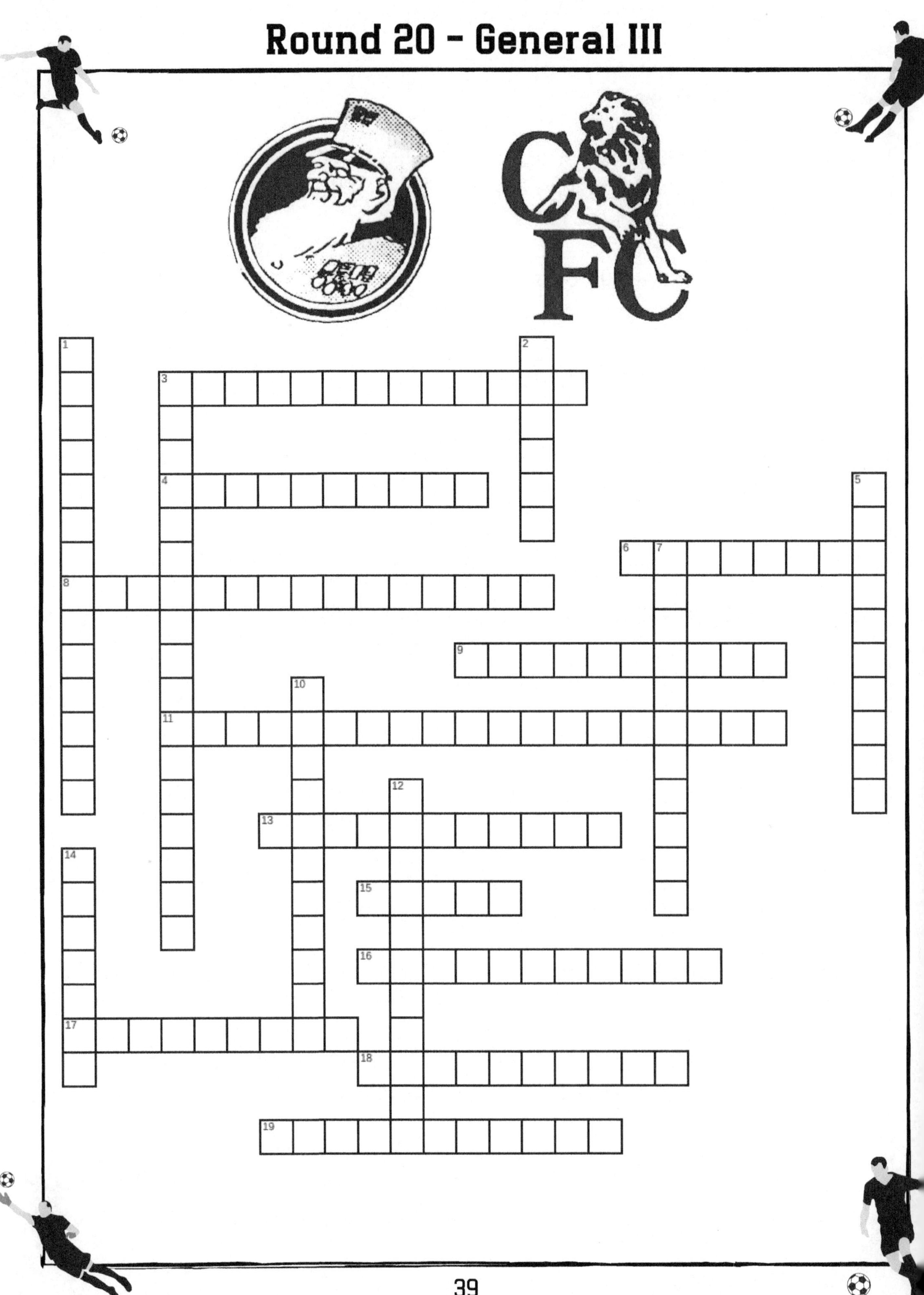

Across

3. First African to win the club's player of the year. (7.6)

4. Coventry striker who was the first player to score a Premier League hat-trick against Chelsea. (4.6)

6. Airline that sponsored Chelsea shirts from 2001-05.

8. Single released in the build-up to the 1972 League Cup Final, with all members of Chelsea's first team squad singing it. (4.2.3.6)

9. Club that Chelsea sold Andriy Shevchenko to in 2009. (6.4)

11. Chelsea's Life President, brother of a famous British nature broadcaster. (7.12)

13. Yugoslavian who won player of the year in 1981. (5.6)

15. Beer brand that sponsored Chelsea shirts from 1994-97.

16. Top goalscorer for Chelsea in the inaugural Premier League season. (4.7)

17. Appointed manager of the Women's side in 2012. (4.5)

18. Former Republic of Ireland and now England international who joined West Ham after being released by Chelsea as a 14-year-old. (6.4)

19. The women's team's home ground, formerly shared with AFC Wimbledon.

Down

1. Scored a brace against Man United on 26th April 2008 to move level on points at the top of the table. (7.7)

2. Club that Édouard Mendy was signed from.

3. Swede who is captain of the Women's side. (9.8)

5. 2021 player of the season. (5.5)

7. Australian goalkeeper who made 7 appearances for the club between 2000-2003. (4.7)

10. Scored the winning goal against Arsenal in the 88th minute to send Chelsea into the Champions League semi-finals. (5.6)

12. Thomas Tuchel's assistant head coach. (4.7)

14. Scored a fantastic, lobbed shot over Víctor Valdés to help send Chelsea through to the 2012 Champions League Final.

Answers

Round 1 - Founding & History

1 THERISINGSUN
2 GUSMEARS
3 GEORGEHILSDON
4 CHARLTONATHLETIC
5 JOHNROBERTSON
6 PARIS
7 DAVIDCALDERHEAD
8 GEORGEMILLS
9 ARGENTINA
10 WINSTONCHURCHILL
11 SHEFFIELDUNITED
12 STOCKPORTCOUNTY
13 WHITE
14 TOTTENHAMHOTSPUR
15 FULHAM
16 ARSENAL
17 BILLYBIRRELL
18 DYNAMOMOSCOW
19 WILLIAMFOULKE
20 MATTBUSBY

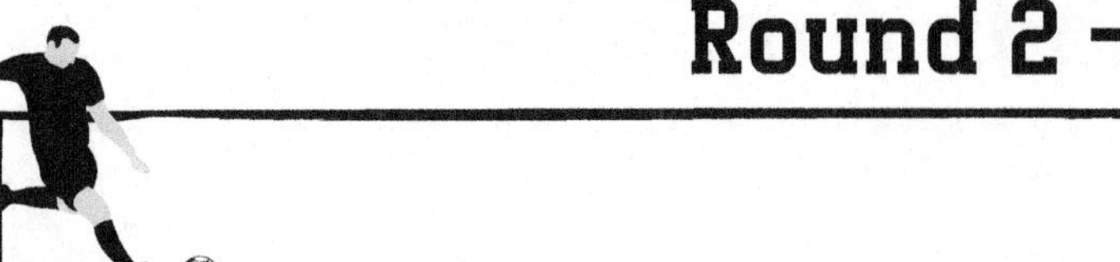

Round 2 - 1950/60s

2. TERRYVENABLES
4. PETERBONETTI
6. CREWEALEXANDRA
12. WOLVERHAMPTONWANDERERS
14. FIFTYTWO
16. DIAMONDS
17. DAVESEXTON
18. LIVERPOOL
19. JIMMYGREAVES

1. TEDDRAKE
2. TOTTENHAMHOTSPUR
3. STGEORGESDAY
5. RONHARRIS
7. KENSHELLITO
8. THEPENSIONER
9. JOHNHOLLINS
10. ROM
11. BOBBYTAMBLING
13. ROYBENTLEY
15. LION

Round 3 - 1970/80s

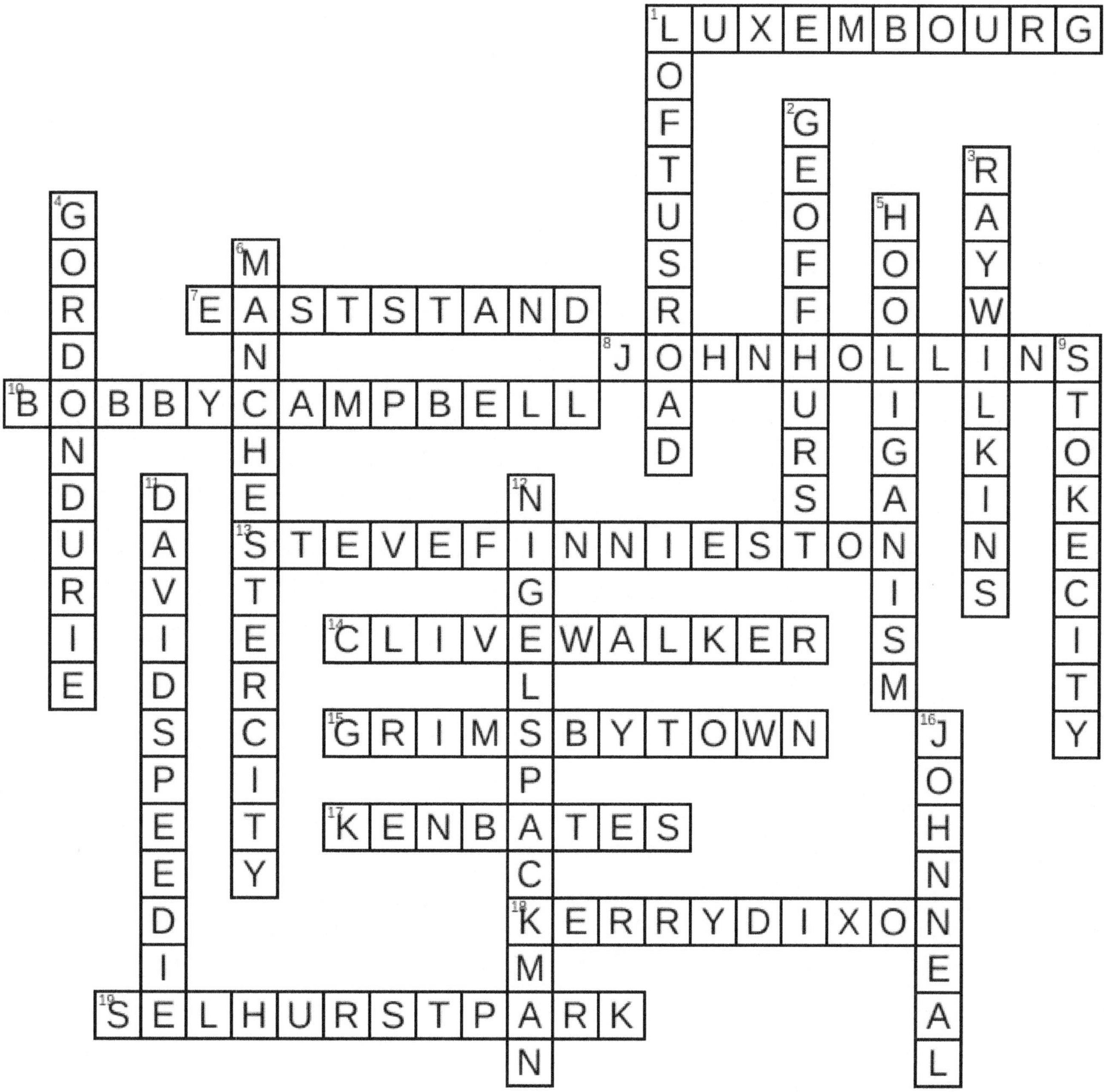

1 LUXEMBOURG
1 LOFTUSROAD
2 GEOFFHURST
3 RAYWILKINS
4 GORDONDURIE
5 HOOLIGANISM
6 MANCHESTERCITY
7 EASTSTAND
8 JOHNHOLLINS
9 STOKECITY
10 BOBBYCAMPBELL
11 DAVIDSPEEDIE
12 NIGELSPACKMAN
13 STEVEFINNIESTON
14 CLIVEWALKER
15 GRIMSBYTOWN
16 JOHNNEAL
17 KENBATES
18 KERRYDIXON
19 SELHURSTPARK

Round 4 - 1990s

1 EDDEGOY
2 DANPETRESCU
2 DENNISWISE
3 DAVIDWEBB
4 IANPORTERFIELD
5 REALZARAGOZA
6 NORWICHCITY
7 GIANLUCAVIALLI
8 REALMADRID
9 MATTHEWHARDING
10 ROBERTODIMATTEO
11 GLENNHODDLE
12 ANDYTOWNSEND
13 FRANKLEBOEUF
14 MIDDLESBROUGH
14 MARKHUGHES
15 GUSPOYET
16 RUUDGULLIT
17 MARKSTEIN
18 STUTTGART

Round 5 - 2000s

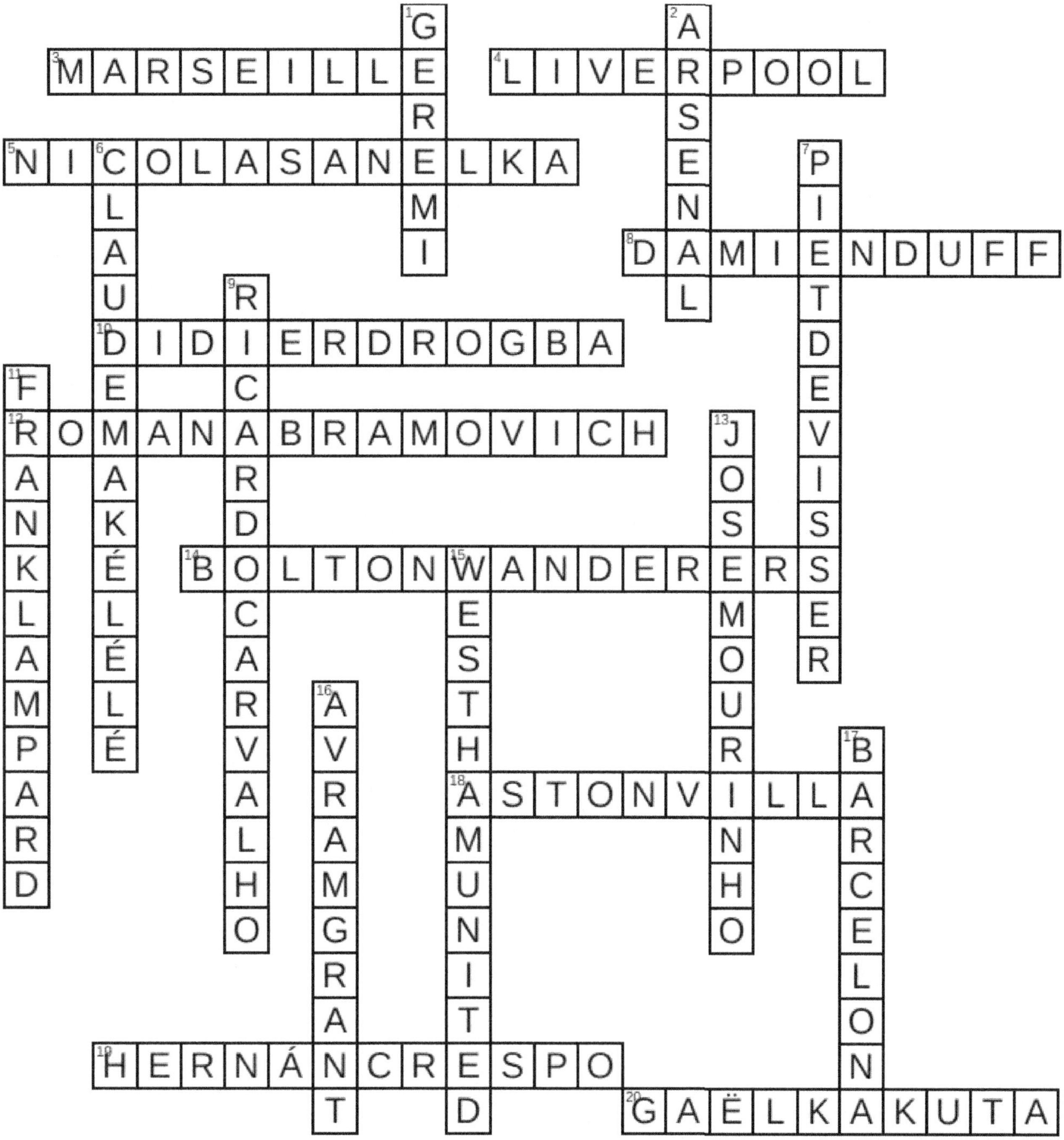

1 GEREMI
2 ARSENAL
3 MARSEILLE
4 LIVERPOOL
5 NICOLASANELKA
6 CLAUDEMAKÉLÉLÉ
7 PIETDEVISSER
8 DAMIENDUFF
9 RICARDOCARVALHO
10 DIDIERDROGBA
11 FRANKLAMPARD
12 ROMANABRAMOVICH
13 JOSEMOURINHO
14 BOLTONWANDERERS
15 WESTHAMUNITED
16 AVRAMGRANT
17 BARCELONA
18 ASTONVILLA
19 HERNÁNCRESPO
20 GAËLKAKUTA

Round 6 - 2010s

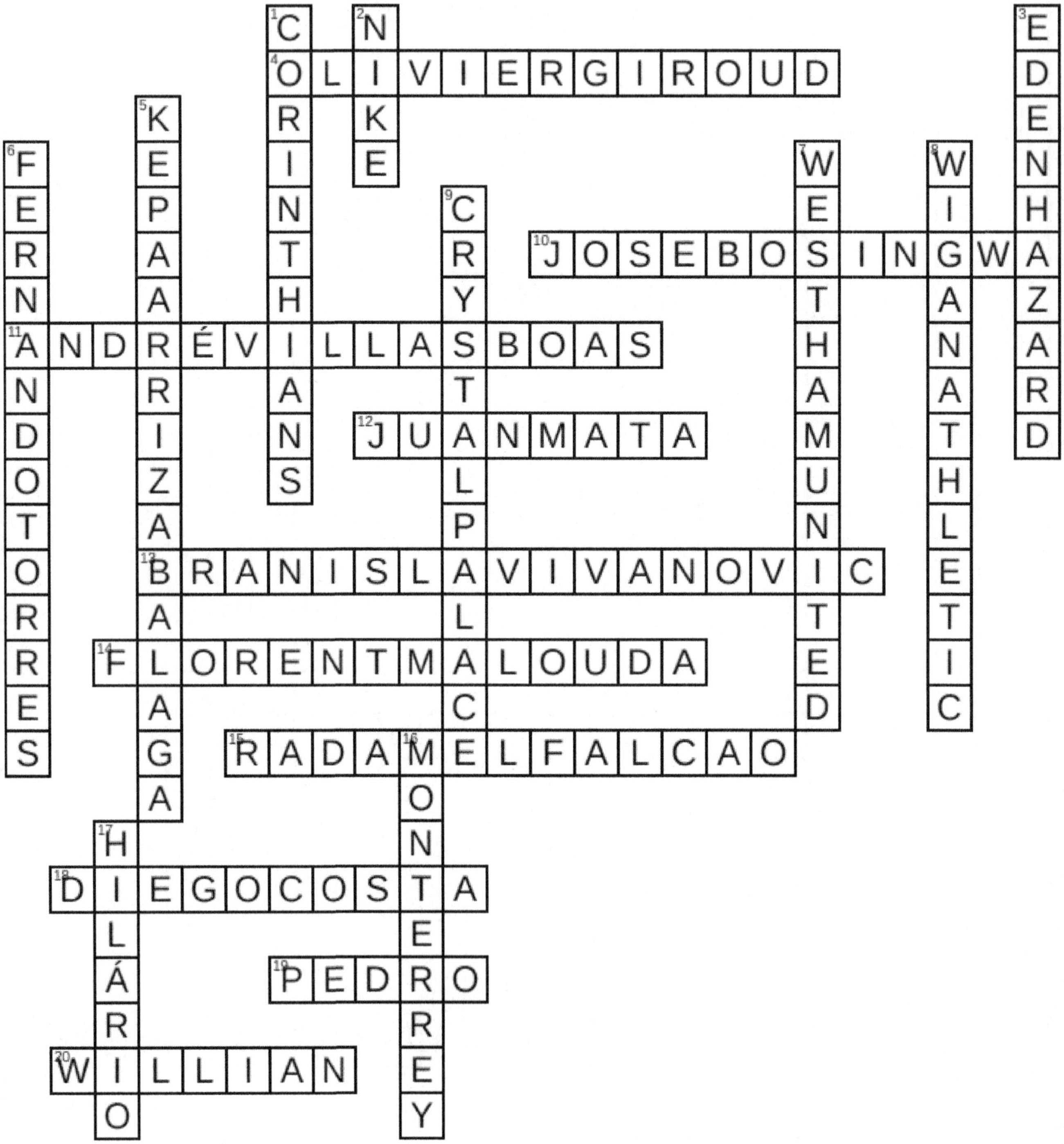

4. OLIVIERGIROUD
10. JOSEBOSINGWA
11. ANDRÉVILLASBOAS
12. JUANMATA
13. BRANISLAVIVANOVIC
14. FLORENTMALOUDA
15. RADAMELFALCAO
18. DIEGOCOSTA
19. PEDRO
20. WILLIAN

1. CORINTHIANS
2. NIKE
3. EDENHAZARD
5. KEPAARRIZABALAGA
6. FERNANDOTORRES
7. WESTHAMUNITED
8. WIGANATHLETIC
9. CRYSTALPALACE
16. MONTERREY
17. HILÁRIO

Round 7 - Champions League 2012 & 2021

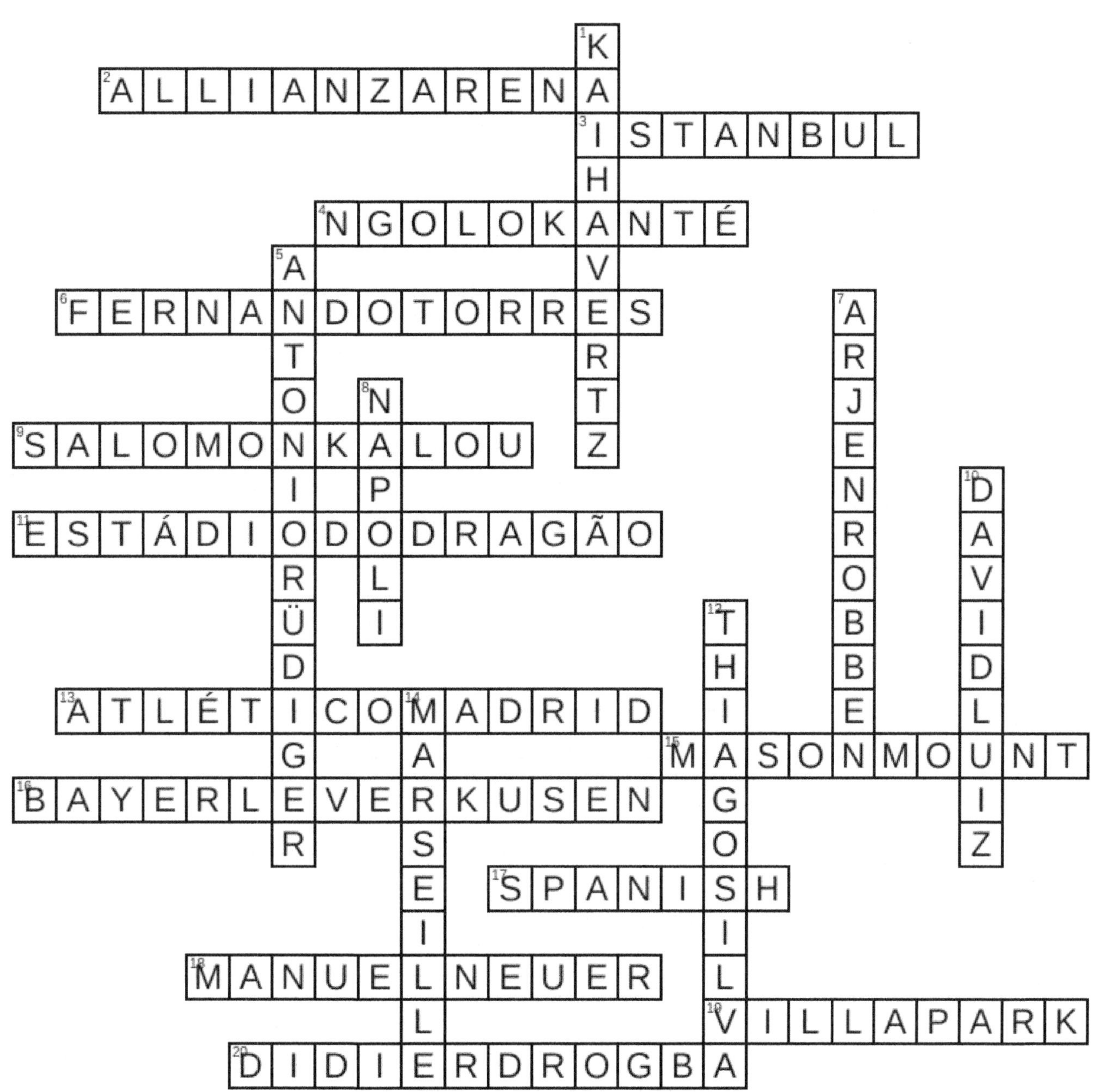

Round 8 - José Mourinho

1. LOUISVANGAAL
2. SANTIAGOBERNABEU
3. WESTHAMUNITED
4. TITOVILANOVA
5. ARSENEWENGER
6. NEMANJAMATIC
7. PAULOFERREIRA
8. ROM
9. MICHAELBALLACK
10. RICARDOCARVALHO
11. THESPECIALONE
12. ANDRIYSHEVCHENKO
13. LIVERPOOL
14. NEWCASTLE
15. JUPPHEYNCKES
16. RUIFARIA
17. LISBO
18. INTERMILAN
19. BOBBYROBSON
20. SUNDERLAND

Round 9 - Italian Managers

1. CUPWINNERSCUP
1. CLAUDIORANIERI
2. CARLOANCELOTTI
3. MANCHESTERUNITED
4. MAURIZIOSARRI
5. RAFAELBENITEZ
6. ANTONIOCONTE
7. ANDREVILLASBOAS
8. YURIZHIRKO
9. WESTBROMWICHALBION
10. MICHYBATSHUAYI
11. JORGINHO
12. GIANLUCAVIALLI
13. ROBERTODIMATTEO
14. ARSENAL
15. JUVENTUS
16. BANKER
17. DAMIENDUFF
18. PORTSMOUTH
19. LEICESTER

Round 10 - Frank Lampard

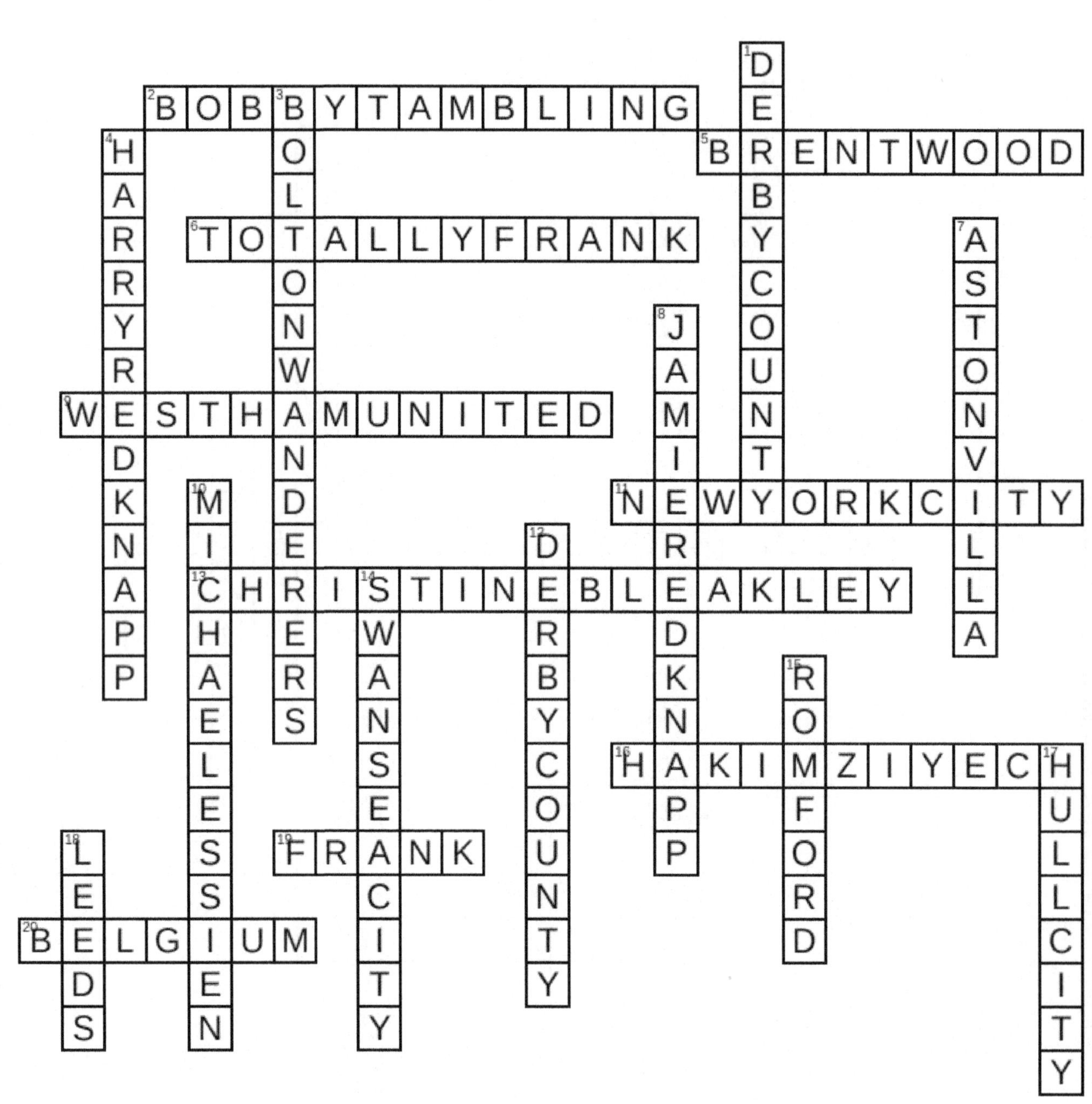

Round 11 - John Terry

Across

2. SPARTAKMOSCOW
3. SCHALKE
5. MARCELDESAILLY
9. ASTONVILLA
12. NOTTINGHAMFOREST
13. READING
14. FULHAM
18. ABOUDIABY
19. ADRIANO
20. JOSEMOURINHO

Down

1. MANCHESTERUNITED
4. BRAZIL
6. ALEXISSANCHEZ
7. SENRAB
8. RIOFERDINAND
10. SUNDERLAND
11. STEVEMCCLAREN
15. UKRAINE
16. BARKING
17. XAVI

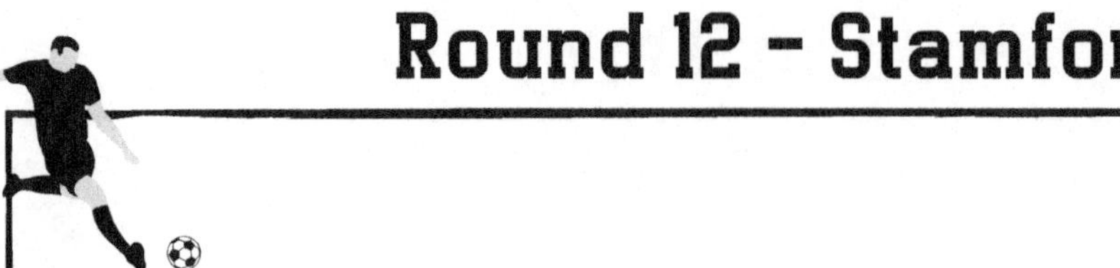

Round 12 - Stamford Bridge

1 MATTHEWHARDING
2 ARCHIBALDLEITCH
3 HUDDERSFIELDTOWN
4 FULHAMROAD
4 FULHAMBROADWAY
5 LONDONMONARCHS
6 CRAVENCOTTAGE
7 PETEROSGOOD
8 WALHAMGREEN
9 STEVECLARKE
10 LONDONATHLETICCLUB
11 JODYMORRIS
12 TAYLOR
13 GEORGEWEAH
14 ARSENAL
15 EARLSCOURT
16 SWITZERLAND
17 SHEDEND
17 SW6
18 BRAZIL

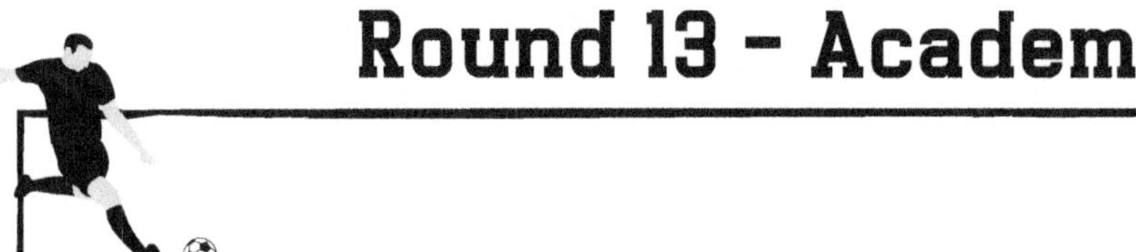

Round 13 - Academy Graduates

1 ROBERTHUTH
2 IANPEARCE
3 NEILCLEMENT
4 JOHNTERRY
5 CRAIGBURLEY
6 LUCASPIAZON
7 GRAHAMSTEWART
8 MASONMOUNT
9 RYANBERTRAND
10 TAMMYABRAHAM
11 MICHAELDUBERR
12 MICHAELMANCIENNE
13 JACKCORK
14 FRANKSINCLAIR
15 REECEJAMES
16 GRAEMELESAUX
17 MUZZYIZZET
18 NATHANAKÉ
19 CARLTONCOLE
20 FIKAYOTOMORI

Round 14 - Club Captains

1 DEREKSAUNDERS
2 FRANKBLUNSTONE
3 FRANKLAMPARD
4 TERRYVENABLES
5 DENNISWISE
6 PETERNICHOLAS
7 NGOLOKANTE
8 MARCELDESAILLY
9 GRAHAMROBERT
10 KENARMSTRONG
11 CÉSARAZPILICUETA
12 COLINPATES
13 JOHNTERRY
14 RONHARRIS
15 GARYCAHILL
16 JORGINHO
17 THIAGOSILVA
18 ROYBENTLEY
19 ANDYTOWNSEND
20 MICKYDROY

Round 15 - Didier Drogba

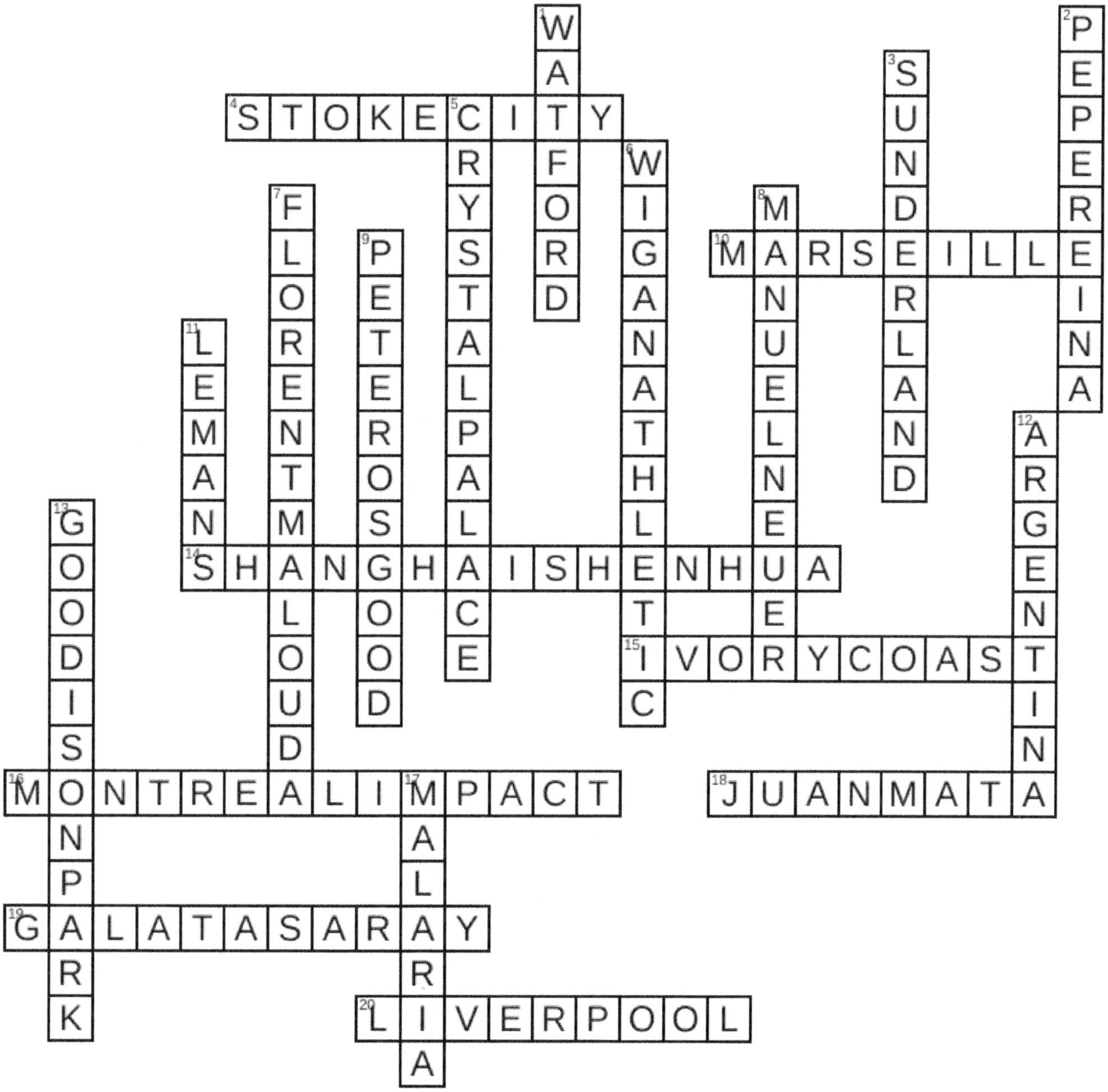

4. STOKECITY
10. MARSEILLE
14. SHANGHAISHENHUA
15. IVORYCOAST
16. MONTREALIMPACT
18. JUANMATA
19. GALATASARAY
20. LIVERPOOL

1. WATFORD
2. PEPEREINA
3. SUNDERLAND
5. CRYSTALPALACE
6. WIGANATHLETIC
7. FLORENTMALOUDA
8. MANUELNEUE
9. PETEROSGOOD
11. LEMANS
12. ARGENTINA
13. GOODISONPARK
17. MALARIA

Round 16 - Gianfranco Zola

1 CLAUDIORANIERI

2 CARLOANCELOTTI

3 RUUDGULLIT

4 ALEXFERGUSON

5 MAURIZIOSARRI

6 EIDURGUDJOHNSEN

7 CAGLIARI

8 TWENTYFIVE

9 PARMA

10 DIEGOMARADONA

11 SARDINI

12 ARRIGOSACCHI

13 WATFORD

14 DERBYCOUNTY

15 MIDDLESBROUGH

16 LIVERPOOL

17 EVERTON

18 WESTHAMUNITED

19 BARCELONA

20 STUTTGART

Round 17 - Eden Hazard

1 PARISSAINTGERMAIN
2 FRANKLAMPARD
3 WATFORD
4 THIBAUTCOURTOIS
5 ANFIELD
6 PAULETA
7 JOSEBOSINGWA
8 SWANSEACITY
9 ARSENAL
10 MANCHESTERUNITED
11 EINTRACHTFRANKFURT
12 THIERRYHENRY
13 CARDIFFCITY
14 JAPAN
15 JUANMATA
16 ZINEDINEZIDANE
17 LILLE
18 NEWCASTLE
19 ENGLAND
20 THORGAN

Round 18 - General I

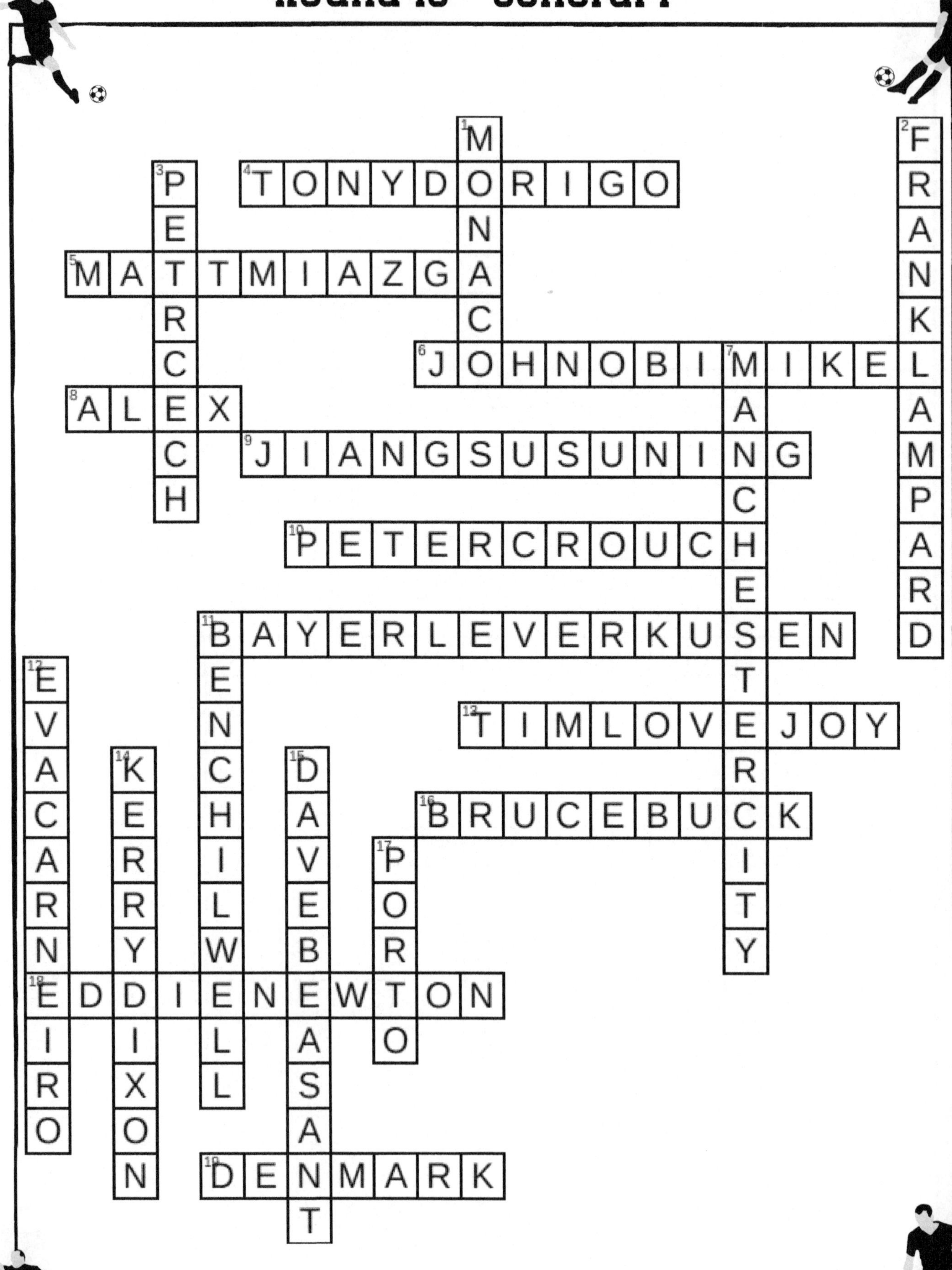

Round 19 - General II

1 INTERMILAN
2 BILLCLINTON
3 HUNGARY
4 TOREANDRÉFLO
5 BARCELONA
6 GIANLUCAVIALLI
7 GAVINPEACOCK
7 GREECE
8 STEVEREDGRAVE
9 PETERBONETTI
10 ARSENAL
11 EDENHAZARD
12 MARCELDESAILLY
13 JOHNTERRY
14 ANDRÉSCHÜRRLE
15 ROYBENTLEY
16 BASEL
17 DIDIERDROGBA
18 OLDTRAFFORD
19 VICTORMOSES

Round 20 - General III

1 MICHAELBALLACK
2 RENNES
3 MICHAELESSIEN
3 MAGDALENAERIKSSON
4 DIONDUBLIN
5 MASONMOUNT
6 EMIRATES
7 MARKBOSNICH
8 BLUEISTHECOLOUR
9 DYNAMOKIEV
10 WAYNEBRIDGE
11 RICHARDATTENBOROUGH
12 ARNOMICHELS
13 PETARBOROTA
14 RAMIRES
15 COORS
16 MICKHARFORD
17 EMMAHAYES
18 DECLANRICE
19 KINGSMEADOW

That's all folks. thank you so much for purchasing this Chelsea crossword book. I really hope you enjoyed it and learnt some cool facts about the club to impress your fellow blues.

As a small independent publisher any reviews you can leave will be a big help as I try to grow my company and produce better and better books for you to enjoy.

If you have any criticisms. please do email me before leaving a negative review and I'd be happy to assist you if you have any problems!

kieran.brown2402@gmail.com

Printed in Great Britain
by Amazon